About Christina

Hi! I think it's always good to give some context... So here is a bit of background on me, Christina Foxwell.

Having been in HR, recruitment, consulting, training and executive leadership for many years, I knew there was something lacking in the corporate world. I felt strongly there was a missed opportunity to engage, equip and make people feel valued and in return, there would ideally be growth, alignment and increased business performance. So with this burning belief, I set up Ignite Purpose in 2012 to support and encourage growth in the clients I work with on a daily basis.

Following my many years of experience in this field, I have seen people step into growth, achieve the unexpected and succeed together. I am, therefore, a firm believer that people can unlock their purpose, joy, development and performance. My work firmly follows the belief that any organisation can achieve a successful high performing culture by engaging in clarity, inclusivity, honesty, clear vision and measurement. In essence, I have based all my research and programs on the delicate balance between people and performance.

As a team at Ignite Purpose we are inspired to grow, learn and step into an uncomfortable place of unlocking change. The change and growth we have seen in leadership teams, cultures and most importantly the people we work with keeps us motivated to continue making a difference.

Along with career development and my own personal growth journey, I have authored two "human stories" which I believe can help all ages understand fundamental issues that are prevalent in everyday life.

On a personal level, I am a mother, grandmother, wife, daughter and sister. I am perfectly imperfect in my life and embrace my story as my gift. The biggest growth piece I continue to learn from is showing vulnerability and staying connected, learning from my world every day and allowing myself to be loved.

Why not connect with me on Linkedin and Facebook? I would love to have you in my world!

Thank you for joining me on this journey. I am passionate about people living their best life, which as I have realised, isn't perfection, it's a daily focus of being our best self in the moment. I am living proof it works. I have written this guide to help support your personal growth, resilience and help you live a more fulfilled and happy life.

Is growing "me" a quick fix? No way, it's going to take effort and a desire to grow! In our work, I have seen many people heal, find focus, be more effective, build great partnership and be very successful. I am sharing these tips with you so that you can do the same in your life. Why share? If I can help make a difference in one person's life a day, I am living my purpose.

How to use this guide? It's simple, schedule time for yourself, I would recommend 20 minutes a day. You are worth it! This is a guide to growth and success and it will take time for you to consider growth and reflect. Just remember "what you give is what you get."

To support you in your journey, you will need to reflect, consider your insights and choose to take action. Our podcast audio guide is also available to aide your growth. See the Resources page at the back of the guide for details on this program

Are you ready? Let's get started!

Christina Foxwell

Step 1

It starts with me

Step 1 Growth starts with me

Ever consider... it starts and ends with "ME". As a performance coach and a person wanting to be more successful or actually just happy; I have to recognise that our ability to live our best life is very much in how we view the world and what we make of it.

In this guide, I will work with you to reflect on how you show up for your world and how you shift your thinking, own your fears and choose to be your best self, today; or at least the best you can muster. I heard someone say we should just be ourselves versus our best self.

I can't agree more. Yet overcoming our fears and putting down our well-forged protection (which has taken you your entire life to create) will require work. Why not consider learning how to be the best of who we really are today.

Why? Because as humans, we were made to be together, and we are wired for connection which ultimately allows us to gain sustenance and joy from our life. When we learn how to grow and embrace who we are, we can be better together, because we are simply ourselves!

A few years ago, I coached a leader who had achieved outstanding "career highlights", and yet they were alone, had no one to share their life with and started suffering health issues. They couldn't understand why others found them hard to be with, yet this leader was constantly pushing for their own worth and was unable to overcome their fear of worthiness.

They were stuck, and they needed to "GROW ME".

For many years, I worked endlessly to prove my worth. I fought hard to show that I was good enough. I achieved so many things, and yet, I was wrestling with ME. I was empty, frustrated, exhausted, hard, judgemental and tough on me and others. My favourite phrase was: "Pull yourself towards yourself". I didn't have time for people who couldn't just get on with things. In fact, in reflection, I was hardest on me. I thought self-development was unnecessary (actually I feared it), and I only needed me and my ability to learn cognitively and power through challenges to win. I had to push myself, and I had to buy my own "story" that I would not be loved and accepted if I didn't achieve. I needed to prove to those who hurt me that I was good enough!

Well, do I have news for me and you out there. My tough exterior was heavy to carry; I was definitely not showing up my best, not able to show those around me the "real me" thereby not living my best life.
I had developed "muscles" to carry my armour; I was STRONG! What had I achieved? I worked my way up to executive leadership, been in global executive teams, managed life as a single parent, moved countries, survived domestic violence, started a successful business, and so much more.

Does it sound like I was living the dream? The answer is NO! I was not. I kept getting caught in similar situations, not good for me! It was the cycles of behaviour and circumstance that I was recreating, with expertise! Every time I overcame, I achieved something new. Every time I came through the cycle, I was less happy, less fulfilled, more shameful, (I will get to shame later). I kept chasing worthiness and happiness; it felt like groundhog day! I wanted to be happy, and yet I didn't know how to get there.

My story The Trigger

About 7 years ago, my husband bought me a book on how to be happy. I was so triggered, yet he was only trying to help me find my way. I should have realised that the trigger was a lighthouse in my stormy sea. My trigger was the warning signal that I was heading for a rocky shore, and I could actually do something about it.

In this guide, you will have moments of "trigger" when you do; I would love you to consider these as lighthouse moments for you. Your trigger signalling where you need to focus, a place where you are stuck. An opportunity to get curious inside yourself to unlock your growth, your best self. Only you have the key to unlock you.

Why grow? I came to a point where It was simply the only way. I needed to go through discomfort, explore it, and be comfortable in it. If I didn't do this, I would keep building armour to protect me, and it would slowly take away all of the best parts of me. The physical toll would steal my health; the mental toll would steal my joy and connection with those in my life. The only opinion was to choose me as a priority.

Today I realise in my darkest days I had been living in fear of not being enough, not being in control, being judged, being alone... I was armoured up. My brain was wired for risk and failure, not opportunity and flow. It felt like a rollercoaster ride. I wanted to be proud of my legacy, and yet I wasn't. Finally, I was absolutely wrestling with setting boundaries. I was sensitive and overthinking... I was getting more stuck and more unhappy. Growing "me" was the only option. I was determined to own my character growth. Not just for me but for my children, my amazing husband and those I love.

Lets get started

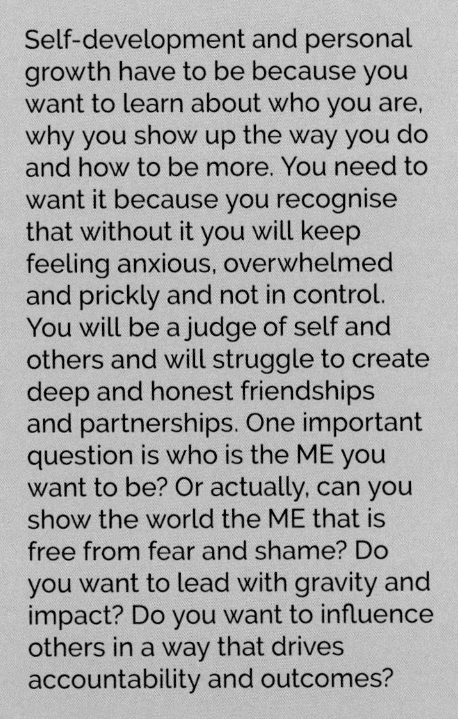

Self-development and personal growth have to be because you want to learn about who you are, why you show up the way you do and how to be more. You need to want it because you recognise that without it you will keep feeling anxious, overwhelmed and prickly and not in control. You will be a judge of self and others and will struggle to create deep and honest friendships and partnerships. One important question is who is the ME you want to be? Or actually, can you show the world the ME that is free from fear and shame? Do you want to lead with gravity and impact? Do you want to influence others in a way that drives accountability and outcomes?

Do you want to LOVE what you do every day? Are you ready to feel more confident, more present, less anxious, more successful in the things that actually matter?
Are you ready to be less angry, resentful and competitive?

Do you want to feel less frustrated and more liberated? Well, it starts with identifying where to start. are you ready to unlock peace and joy?

I have a small check-list I would love you to reflect on. If you could shift any of these things which would you choose to work on?

- Needing to be in control
- Overcoming procrastination
- Worrying about what others think of me
- Being a perfectionist
- Always comparing myself to others. Being constantly anxious
- Struggling to connect with others Doubting myself
- Workaholic and always "being on" Frustrated with others

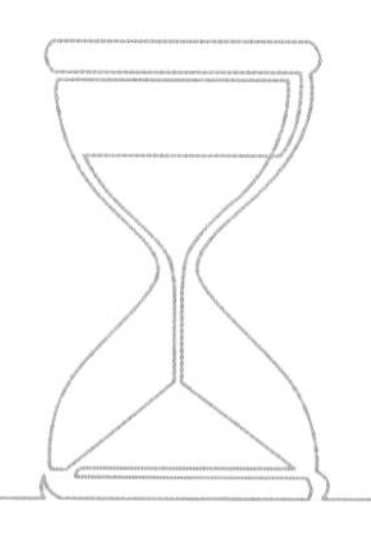

Reflection will be a large part of your growth and learning. Embracing being "comfortable" in discomfort will help you live a life you are proud of surrounded by the people you love and those who enrich your life.

How do you reflect? It starts with your ability to consider, understand, accept and own, and then choose to do something different.

Let's start at the beginning, are there any areas in the list on the previous page you want to work on? (I would recommend only choose 2 - 3 max). You may also write down a few of your own if I haven't captured the areas you want to focus on.

Reflection

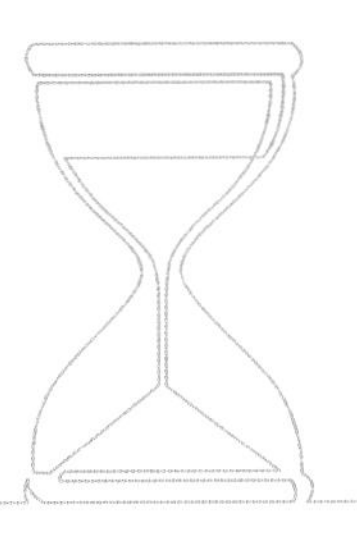

Why have you chosen these areas?

Reflection

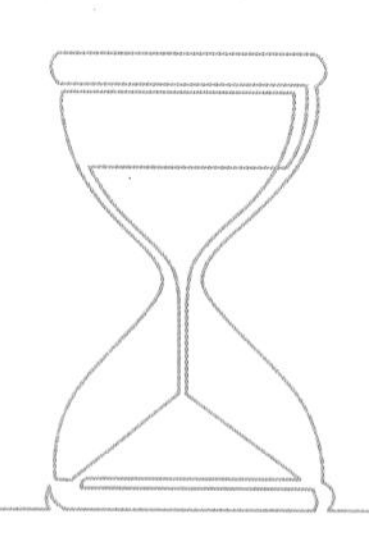

When you are in these "growth" areas, how are you showing up? What do others see in you and what impact do you have?

How do you feel when you are in this state?

Reflection

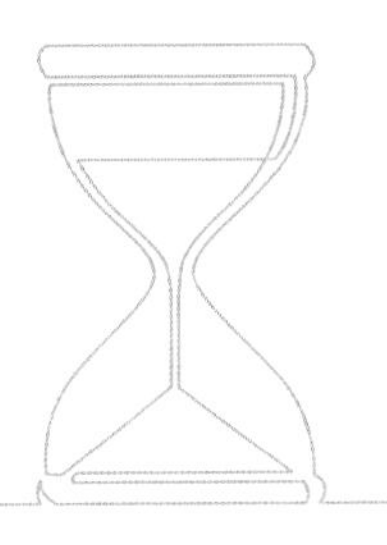

If you could shift how you show up, what would you like your impact to be? Why is it important to you?

An important note to consider is that if you are feeling guilty, don't. Guilt is an emotion that doesn't serve us. It keeps us stuck. Rather focus on who you are, choose to work on whom you want to be and grow.

Step 2

What can you control?

Step 2 The fight for control

"It's not what you say to everyone else that determines your life; it's what you whisper to yourself that has the greatest power" - Marcandangel. Our mind has power; we need to rewire our self-talk to find our way through!

"You may not be able to control every situation and its outcome, but you can control your attitude and how you deal with it." So how we respond to the things outside of our control matters.

Both quotations challenge the "self" in us and highlight the things that we can't control. Let me use a life example that I hope you will relate too.

I have two children, and raising kids isn't for the fainthearted. Imagine trying to get out the front door on time while your strong-willed teenager takes their time to dress, and eat breakfast? If you live in a large city like Sydney, it takes an hour or more to get anywhere in peak hour traffic. You know that you will be late if you don't leave at a certain time. You want to control the situation and yet you can't. You want to control your teenager and to scream and to yell makes them slow down even more. If you are anything like me, you would be boiling over right about now! When you eventually drive off the tension in the car is thick, and you can hardly breathe. You don't speak until you stop at school.
You are late for your meeting; you are uptight and less than "present". Your defenses are still up from the fear of not being in control of that horrible reality that you will not make it on time. You lose the opportunity to influence, engage and align.

Of course, the only thing we can control is how we respond, prepare, and then do our best while we are in the moment.

What can you control?

I am sure you must have your own story of control? Let's talk about 2020, shall we? How many of us had plans to go on a wonderful holiday, get married, see parents, run a successful business, get a promotion? Maybe we lost a loved one? For some of us, things we wanted haven't happened, and things we didn't want to happen did. Our world has been so different from what we anticipated. The lesson of what we actually are in control of is profound.

We can't control the environment ... We can't control others; we can only control how we show up and connect with people to be the best influencers and to engage positive outcomes.

In reality, that means we need to learn how to find our way with others, not operate from a place of consistent need to be in control, to find a way to have strong mutual partnerships. It means we might need to check our intent when we feel the need to control and get clear about why we want to control, what it means to us. What are we telling ourselves when we need to wrestle for control? Is it true or is it simply our fear and protection kicking in?

We need each other and we are better together. So if we always thought we had control over others and our environment and now we realise that we don't, where do we start shifting and changing?

I think you will know the answer to this question. The change starts in us, in the self. It starts in how we think, what we say and how we do things. It starts because we choose it, and we recognise that our journey will be filled with moments of "failure". So "choice" is my act of control. The choice to be more than I am or maybe it's the choice to **BE ALL I AM!**

Circles of control

Fighting for and to control is exhausting, it takes effort, and we defiantly don't bring the best of who we are. People experience the prickly part of our "armour" (How we have learnt to protect ourselves - how we show up when in fear) and we get frustrated over circumstances and actions that aren't in our control to change. Why not consider the model below. Think about your world right now and what frustrates you. Are you in control?

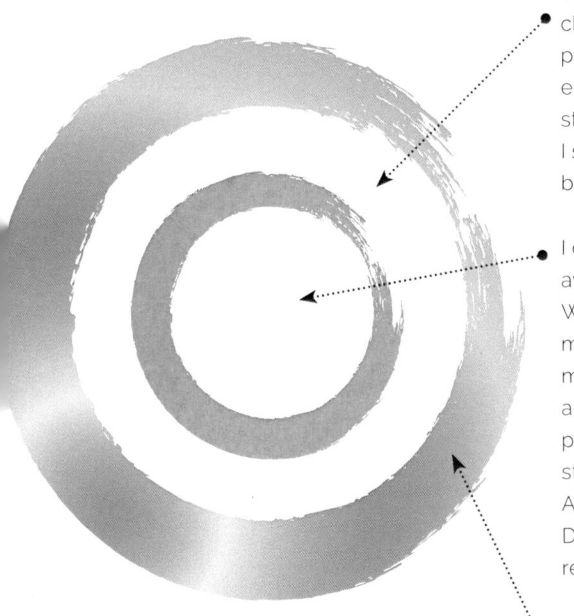

Whom do I need to influence? What relationships do I have and cherish?How do I learn about perspective, listen deeply and engage with honesty? Work on staying open to others? How do I support vs fix others?How do I become a great partner?

I directly control me. I need to be aware of my thinking and actions. What language do I use? What is my emotional state? What does my body language say? What am I telling myself? Am I taking perspective?Where am I getting stuck? Am I present in the now? Am I worried about tomorrow? Do I live in fear that the past will repeat itself?

What is outside of my control and influence? What do I need to accept?What do I need to let go of? What fear is holding me in the cycle of control that is negatively impacting me?

Reflection

What things outside of your control frustrate you? Do you need to work on letting go? Is worrying about it impacting your sense of self-worth, your relationships and even your health?

Who are the key relationships in your world that you need to find alignment and partnership with? List the names of the key people and then consider which ones need more connection?

Reflection

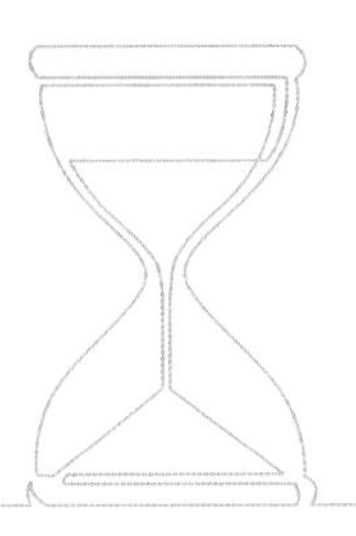

How self-aware are you? How are you showing up for your life? What are the 5 great character traits you have - that help you get along and support others? What are your 5 most challenging character traits that impact others negatively (Especially when you are not in control)?

What are your reflections on showing up your best self?

Step 3

Understanding my mindset!

Step 3 My mindset...

I need to be willing to grow, and it starts with my mindset!

How many of you are having to take a few deep breaths right now. When I first realised I needed to grow who I was, I had heart palpitations!

Actually, what I needed to do was be vulnerable, and boy that was not part of my MO! Vulnerable people freaked me out. Actually, I saw them as victims. Yes, victims are very likely to be on the vulnerability scale, yet, being vulnerable means I am willing to try something new without knowing the outcome. I am willing to be emotionally exposed. The second of these is my Achilles-heel. I didn't want to be seen as a failure or weak, so I had to "armour up" and be strong.

I had experienced such hurt in my life that no way did I want to go anywhere near being emotionally too exposed or, being open. In actual fact, I felt being open or vulnerable would take away from my strength. Yet this mindset kept me small; it held me captive... and the walls of "strength" I had built were slowly crushing my joy, happiness and connection to my world. I needed to grow I didn't have a choice.

In my first session with my coach/ therapist, Robby asked me what I wanted to work on. I remember saying, I wanted to work on being Free. Free from crushing anxiety, worry, trying to be strong, being in control, not failing, being "perfect". Actually, I needed to be free from the stories I was telling myself.

This is exactly what I did! It unlocked ME! I had to start with my mindset and how I thought because my mindset defined my ability to take perspective and grow. I still work on my mindset, its a life journey.

Growth Mindset
Carol Dweck

Carol Dweck is a researcher who studies human motivation. She has studied why some people succeed and why others don't. Her model helps us understand the continuum of growth mindset and a fixed mindset. The most effective and successful people have a Growth Mindset. We are all on a continuum of Fixed and Growth based on our life experiences. This is your growth guide, so it would be great to reflect on your growth areas in this continuum.

FIXED MINDSET	**GROWTH MINDSET**

I need to look credible and be accepted	I need to learn from experiences
As a result: I may plateau and achieve less than my full potential	**As a result:** I reach even higher levels of achievement

How does vulnerability come into this model? When I am vulnerable (Growth Mindset), I am willing to be exposed, to fail, to try. I am actually open, and I am growing. When I am wrestling with vulnerability (Fixed Mindset), I struggle with failure and am worried I might not be good enough (to be accepted).

Vulnerability

CLOSED Excruciating Vulnerable	← →	**OPEN** Vulnerable
Fear of failing.. being rejected... not being good enough		Courage to try, to fail, to be less than perfect, to be exposed

Growth Mindset

Carol Dweck

FIXED MINDSET		GROWTH MINDSET

Avoid Challenges	*Challenges*	Embrace Challenges
Gives up easily	*Obstacles*	Persist in the face of setbacks
See effort as fruitless or my own failing	*Effort*	See effort as the path to mastry
Ignore useful feedback I see it as critism	*Feedback*	Take on feedback and reflect on growth
I am threatened by the success of others (Competing)	*Success of others*	Find inspiration and growth in the success of others

Reflection My mindset

We all show up differently in different situations. I never thought I had a fixed mindset, yet the more "armor" I wore to be strong, the more fixed I became. I had to reflect on how and why I was responding negatively to different situations with people. I thought I was definitely a growth mindset person yet when discomfort hit me; I was not as open as I thought I was! So here is your time to reflect. Why don't you rate yourself on the scale below?

Consider the scales below and the key areas of growth you selected earlier in this guide. When you are in your growth areas, how do you respond to Challenges, Obstacles, Effort, Feedback, and Success? (eg. do you avoid challenges or embrace them?)

MOST TIMES	SOMETIMES	HARDLY EVER		HARDLY EVER	SOMETIMES	MOST TIMES
I AVOID CHALLENGES			*Challenge*	I EMBRACE CHALLENGES		
I GIVE UP EASILY			*Obstacles*	I PERSIST IN THE FACE OF SET-BACKS		
I SEE EFFORT AS FRUITLESS OR MY OWN FAILING			*Effort*	I SEE EFFORT AS THE PATH TO MASTRY		
I IGNORE USEFUL FEEDBACK I SEE IT AS CRITISM			*Feedback*	I TAKE ON FEEDBACK AND REFLECT ON GROWTH		
I AM THREATENED BY THE SUCCESS OF OTHERS (COMPETING)			*Success of others*	I FIND INSPIRATION AND GROWTH IN THE SUCCESS OF OTHERS		

Reflection

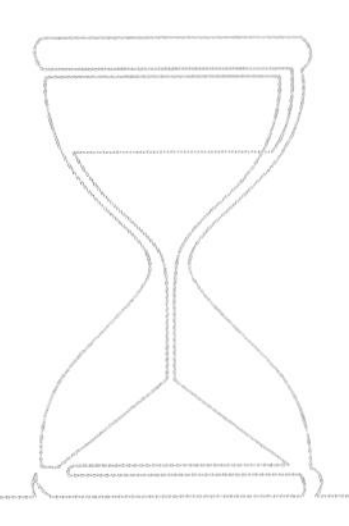

Based on your reflections, what have you learnt about yourself? How can you stay present and recognise when you slip into a fixed mindset? Why do you think you shift into your fixed mindset? What do you tell yourself when you are in this space? How can you change this story and allow yourself to be more open?

Step 4

To grow or not to grow. My choice

Step 4 My choice to grow

Several years ago a friend said to me "You can't give what you don't have". Ever heard of this statement? It profoundly unlocked my choice to grow, how could I teach leadership when I couldn't lead me, after all, leading who we are is the foundation for leading others.

I had taught "me" to rise through my past vs stand in my presence in my career and life. What do I mean? Well, I was using my experience as my reason to rise and prove my worth. I was independent and needed to show up strong, self-reliant and tough. Of course, it allowed me to rise, and I am so grateful for this part of my life. Yet, it was a lonely and fearful existence.

The tougher I became, the less I allowed others to stand next to me. My mindset was that I didn't need a coach, someone who had not walked the stony path of life as I had (that was the story I told myself). Why would I open myself to judgment? Why would I show weakness? I didn't want to be exposed. I must say I am proud of what I achieved and how hard I worked. Yet, I realise the toll it took on me. I was living in a constant state of survival. I was in a fixed mindset!

Fast-forward to today... I have had a coach for a few years now. Actually, I had a "therapist" coach first, and now I have an executive coach based in Canada. I love it! I am present in myself. I am choosing my growth daily, I am learning about me, I am leading me, I am failing at times and standing up with grace. I am no longer chasing worthiness, yet I am plugged into purpose. Presence allows me to be here, now, use what I have, be wise, be a guide, hold the space for others and be the best I can be today. It's a daily choice. A choice that continues to unlock freedom for me!

Shifting your mindset

To grow or not to...

We can all fear growth because growth could have a negative "story" for us. As you start this journey understanding your fears and barriers to growth will help you step through discomfort and unlock your potential, to live your best life, only you can do it.

Here is your first reflection; I have identified three high-level growth fears and would like you to consider how they relate to your "story" the one you could be telling yourself to stay safe (in a Fixed mindset).

You might think of a few other fear stories besides the ones I mention, and you will be able to write these down during your reflection.

1 YOU ARE UNWILLING TO FACE CHANGE

Some people fear growth because they know it will bring up areas where they need to make changes. Whether that is personal or professional, the goal of growth is improved performance, enjoying life, feeling fulfilled ... and that means you have to be willing to change your beliefs and change your actions in some areas of your life.

"You can't go back and change the beginning, but you can start where you are and change the ending" - C.S. Lewis

If you don't believe that change is necessary, you won't believe you need growth. You would be wrong.

The very best performers in every human endeavor work on who they are and how they show up. Their core belief is that, if they change something, they can perform at an even higher level.

They don't compete with others; they work on how they can be better at what they do, at who they are. They can make a greater impact in their world, and they live a happier and more fulfilled life. They don't shy away from trying something new.

2 YOU ARE AFRAID "GROWTH" MEANS YOU AREN'T CAPABLE

Growth "enablers" like reflection, feedback and coaching do not mean that you aren't a capable individual. It does not mean that you don't have the ability or the resources to achieve your performance goals and live a fulfilling life.

Growth isn't a negative reflection on you as a person. Growth is an indication that you ARE "capable". It's evidence that someone (maybe you) believe that you can gain new insights and perform better with some insight and ideas.

No one invests in "growth" programs when they believe that they are hopeless. No company invests in Growth programs for their people when they believe those people aren't "capable". Investment of time, commitment and money unlock great potential in the future for the person being coached and the people that work and live alongside the person growing.

3 YOU ARE AFRAID "GROWTH" MEANS YOU AREN'T CAPABLE

This one is a biggie. It's the deep-seated issue that prevents many people from embracing Growth. Some people don't want to be held accountable for changing.

They don't like to acknowledge the difference between what they say and what they do. More than anything, they don't want to have to answer to someone; they'd rather hide from their problems, their challenges. They will often justify the reason for not being accountable. People that live their best and most fulfilled life embrace accountability. They recognise that in all things they have some responsibility. They accept it for what it is and then work on being more.

They fearlessly look at and own the gaps in their performance, whom they want to be and how they show up and impact others.

They look at "reflection" and even coaching as an accountability process. They expect tough questions, and difficult reflections to help expand what they believe is possible and capable of.

They understand that when they get "triggered" or really uncomfortable, it's their moment to be accountable and really curious about themselves. It's the moment to accept and own it!

"Accepting complete responsibility for your life means you refuse to make Excuses or blame others for anything in your life that you aren't happy about." - Brian Tracy

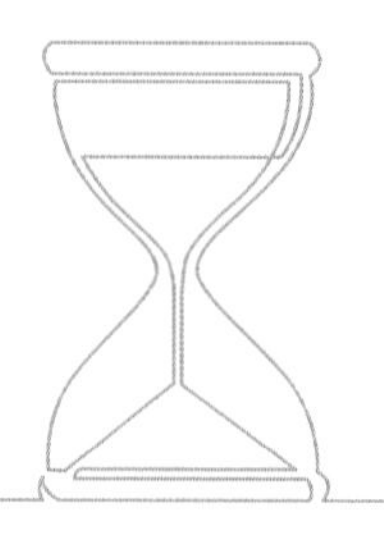

My greatest fear was to be judged as not good enough and to be left out. My other fears have been that I don't have enough and need to be STRONG to survive. These fears and the armor it created held me back from growth, coaching and living my best life. I am now working every day on me, it's allowing me to live with purpose and joy.

What fear "stories" do you need to acknowledge that keep you from growth? ** The things you tell yourself when you are trying to be strong!

Reflection

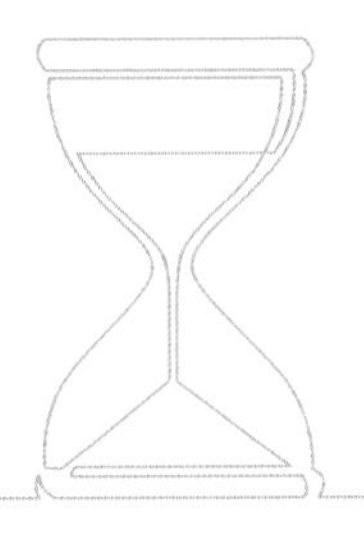

How do these fears show up in your behaviours or mindset?

What would a happier more fulfilled YOU look like?

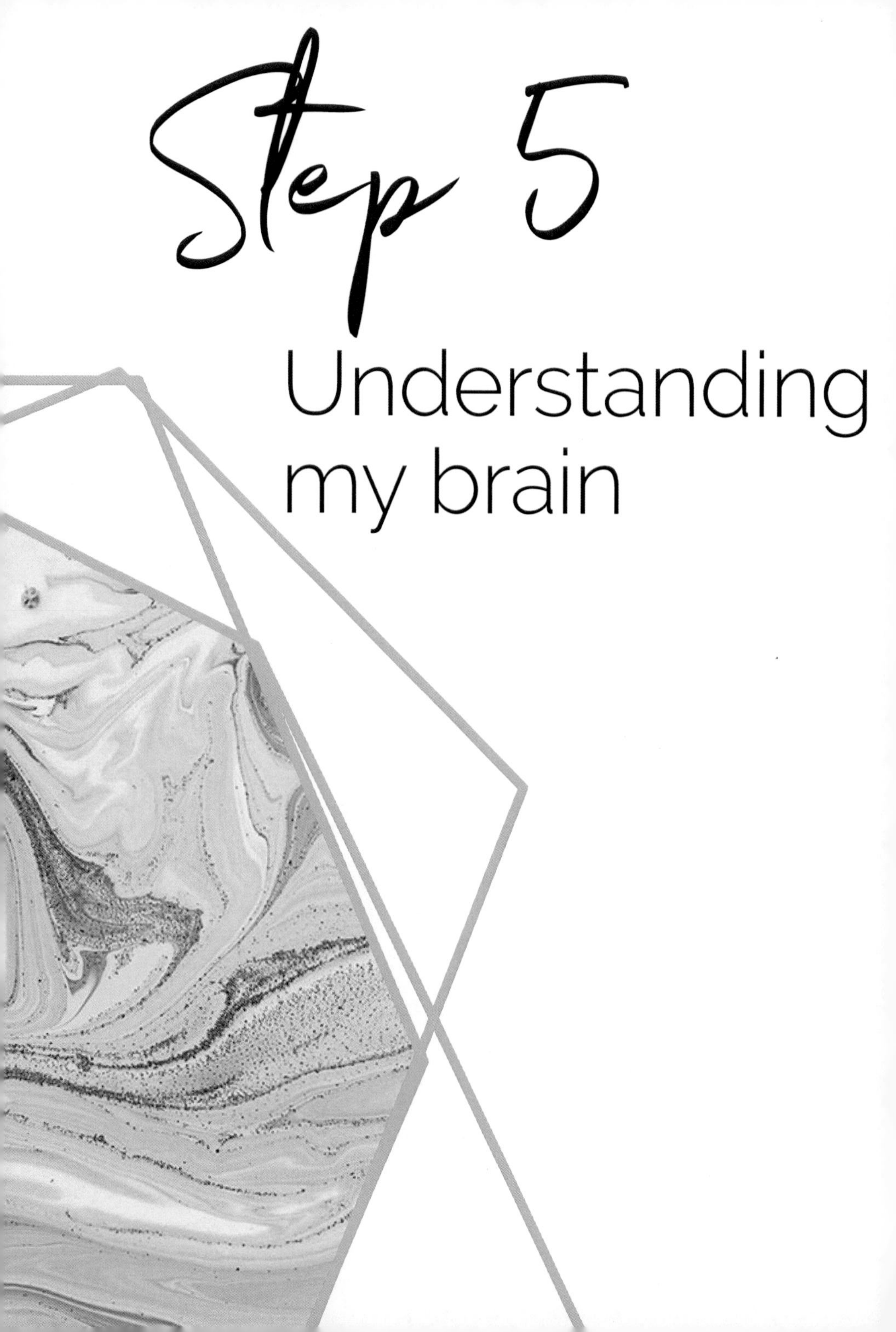

Step 5

Understanding my brain

Step 5 I know I need to grow. What now?

So by now, you have started realising that growing "ME" is an interesting journey and that the only way to really unlock your own potential is to do it yourself. Reflecting on the areas you need to work on is the start. Now we are going to reflect on the tools to consider; like how to rewire your mindset, your beliefs and your actions. Let's start with your Brain!

Two years ago I was in family counselling with my son and who had been bullied at school. During one session, I was trying to be so STRONG! The psychologist called me after the session and shared with me that I was suffering from Trauma, and that is was an opportunity area for me. WOW! I got so triggered! Yet, I choose to find a Coach who helped me transform my mind. In my life, I had learnt how to BE STRONG, and I had been operating in my survival brain—a beautiful place to nurture a fixed mindset.

I was exhausted, and I was operating in a continual stress Zone! I thought I was in a great place, yet I was in a "fear" space of proving my worthiness, and I was not my best self. The self I wanted to be!So let's talk about our brain, shall we?

Are you stuck in survival brain

How often do we slip into "survival brain"? When we see our world as unsafe, we are not in control, it's painful? Our survival mode kicks in to protect us.

Based on our story and on how we have grown up, we can get triggered into survival brain for so many reasons. Our Survival Brain is our old brain or to make it really simple, the behavioural instincts of prehistoric man. Imagine, we live in the prehistoric days.

Our brains back then were still evolving. When we saw something that could be dangerous - a threat, our Emotional Brain would realise we were in trouble, and our Survival Brain would Trigger! (I refer to this a POP/pufferfish moment). Three things could happen:

Fight - Attack the threat with all you have

Flight - Run and hide from the threat to stay safe

Freeze - Pretend you are dead so that the threat will go away

When we are under perceived threat, brain scans have shown that cortical blood flow is redirected into our Survival Brain to give it all the resources needed to help keep us safe. So for those of us who have been raised in survival brain, it might be time to disconnect and reconnect. Why not do a quick stress test...

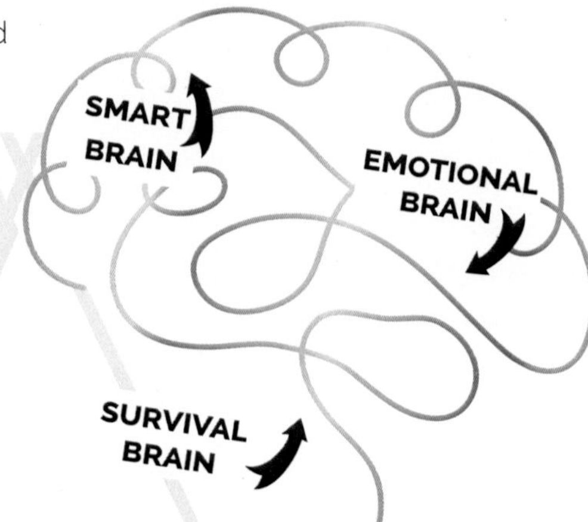

Stress test- Survival Brain

This stress test will help you consider if your "Survival Brain" might be triggered and if this could possibly cause wellness challenges.

Life event	Score
Death of a spouse	100
Divorce	73
Marital Seperation	65
Imprisonment	63
Death of a close family member	63
Personal injury or illness	53
Marriage	50
Dismissal from Work	47
Marital Reconciliation	45
Retirement	45
Change in health of family member	44
Pregnancy	40
Sexual difficulties	39
Gain a new family member	39
Business readjustment	39
Change in financial state	38
Death of a close friend	37
Change to different line of work	36
Change in frequency of arguments	35
Major mortgage	32
Foreclosure of mortgage or loan	30
Change in responsibilities at work	29
Child leaving home	29
Trouble with in-laws	28
Outstanding personal achievement	26
Spouce starts or stops work	26
Begin or end School	26
Change in living	25
Revision of Personal Habits	24
Trouble with your employer	23
Change in working conditions	20
Change in residence	20
Change in schools	20
Change in recreation	19
Change in Social activities	18
Minor Mortgage or loan	197
Change in sleeping habits	16
Family Reunions	15
Change in eating Habits	15
Vacations	13
Major religious holidays	12
Minor violation of the law	11

Consider your last 12 months. What are the key life events you have experienced? Add up your life event weighting....

SCORE OF 300+ Risk of Burnout, illness and mental fatigue

SCORE OF 150 -299 Moderate Risk of Burnout, illness and mental fatigue

SCORE OF LESS THAN 150 Slight Risk of Burnout, illness and mental fatigue

Reflection

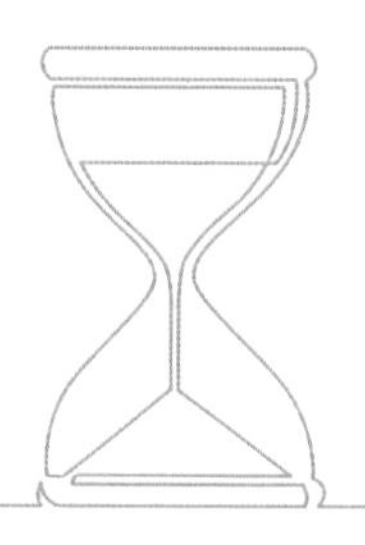

How did you score on the stress test? What insights do you have?

We all get triggered at times (Flight, fight or freeze). What does this look like for you? (The trigger and the emotion?)

Reflection

What fears trigger for you when you go into survival brain?

What do you tell yourself when you are feeling stressed and triggered? How are you showing up?

Reflection

Is the fear story that you are telling yourself the full story?
Is the story one that is telling you to armour up?
What do you need to understand about your story?

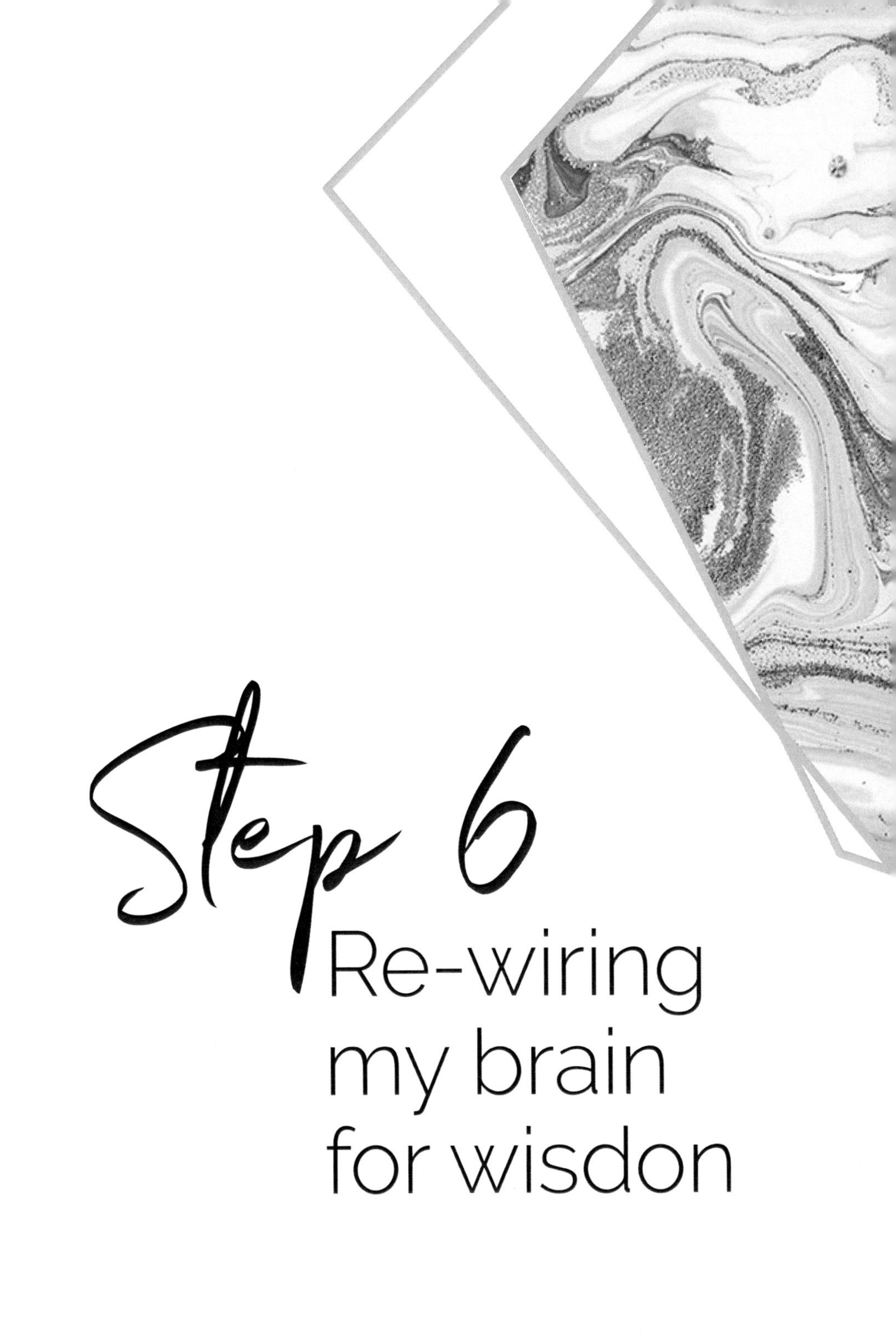

Step 6

Re-wiring my brain for wisdon

Shifting my brain towards positive

Shawn Achor's research is captured in his book The Happiness Advantage. Happiness is relative, yet our happiness or I would even rephrase happiness as "being present as a person" is our core, and our success revolves around it. Here are a few facts from his research:

1 .Meditation studies show that 5 minutes of mediation is enough to start wiring your brain for calm and contentment.

2. A calm brain means we start living with HOPE and a desire to look forward to tomorrow vs fear tomorrow.

3. We can infuse positivity in our surroundings and start accepting things for what they are

4. Learn to embrace failures as a stepping stone when we fail: instead of getting caught in the downward spiral of fear and overcompensation and catastrophising. We stand in the discomfort, embrace ourselves, accept it and choose to learn from it.

So, why don't we "myth bust" success. The best job in the world or fame and fortune won't make you feel free, happy and fulfilled. Happiness is based on 10% of our environment, and 90% is based on our perspective. We need 'practices' to help us shift our perspectives which mean we engage our smart brain and build wisdom. We learn how to wire our brain for opportunity and joy! We need to learn to enjoy it now!

Happiness is the joy we feel while striving for our potential (the journey!)

Rewriting my brain!

Building wisdom

When I realised I was living in a constant state of "Survival Brain". I recognised that I was overwhelmed with anxiety, yet I had learned how to use this "state" to power my career and business forward. I was slowly feeling more and more overwhelmed; then I stumbled across Shawn Achor's work.

I also started looking into Neuroplasticity to calm my brain to plug into wisdom and my "Smart Brain". I wanted to show up the "best me" for my family, friends, and beautiful clients I serve. I loved Shawn's TED Talk on the Happiness Advantage. Why not check it out?

To help you shift your thinking, plug into your "Smart Brain", feel positive, feel centred... try the following for a month.
(I would choose 2 practices to start)

EXERCISE
If you could do 15 minutes of Cardio a day. You train your brain that your behaviour matters.

GRATITUDE
Three gratitudes a day for 21 Days. Train your mind to scan for positives instead of threats ("Survival Brain").

JOURNAL
Write down one positive experience you have had during the last 24 hours. It teaches your brain to relive it and that behaviour matters.

KINDESS TO OTHERS
Random acts of kindness and not expecting a return. Writing a letter, note or email to someone thanking them for what they have done in your life.

MEDITATE
Spending time to "quiet your mind". Doing breathing exercises, use the CALM app and practicing acceptance and letting go of fear

DEEPEN SOCIAL CONNECTIONS
Connection is why we are here Deeper connection with others allow us to feel a sense of belonging. This allows us to feel we can be who we are and are not judged.

Re-wiring my brain

Today's learning will mean choosing to do things differently and shifting your brain into your Smart or wise brain where it can be more present and open to learn, explore and understand. Where you can see opportunities, find solutions and be your best imperfect self.

Eckhart Tolle, the author of The power of now, writes; "The mind is essentially a survival machine. Attack and defence against other minds, gathering, storing, and analyzing information. This is what it is good at, but it is not at all creative. All true artists, whether they know it or not, create from a place of no-mind, from inner stillness. The mind then gives form to creative impulse and INSIGHT. Even the greatest scientists have reported that their creative break came at a time of mental quietude."

To support your practices, I would encourage you to mark this chapter of the guide and return to it daily for 21 days or to journal separately to this guide. These practices will take a bit of additional time in your day, yet they are so worth it. We need to find ways to calm the mind/ brain to be open for a growth mindset and the learning we want to embrace. We need the learning pathways in our brain to light up. We need our wise brain to be switched on more regularly.

It's a practice of caring for yourself, learning not to believe everything your brain (mind) tells you, and knowing when to disconnect so that you can reconnect in the now. Short circuit thinking no longer reliving yesterday or fearing tomorrow by being here now.

Reflection Gratitude practice

Appreciate everything

This practice starts with being grateful for small things, not only the BIG life events or things. Looking around you and recognising the simple things. The sunshine, a hug from your child, a text message from a friend ...

Be grateful in your challenges

Being grateful in the toughest times isn't easy. Yet there is always something to acknowledge. My dad died this year. It was heartbreaking. I remember after the funeral we all dialled into a family virtual call and we started being grateful for what he meant in our lives and how wonderful it was to be together.

Practice Mindfulness

Sitting down daily for 6-8 weeks practising mindful gratitude will help rewire your brain patterns that will develop more empathy and happiness. You do this by sitting still, closing your eyes and visualising what you are grateful for. Consider how it makes your body feel.

Practice Mindfulness

Post your mindfulness reflections, why not journal how you feel and what you are grateful for. Write down your positive thoughts. Don't do this quickly, why not be conscious about the words you use and how you are retelling any fear stories.

Reflection Meditation practice

Spend time to "quiet your mind". Do breathing exercises, use the CALM app, practice acceptance and let go of fear... if you can, use your hourglass... Staying present allows me to live NOW... not be stuck in the past or worry about the future...

Sit comfortably

- Take a seat - sit comfortably not perching
- Make sure your feet touch the floor or are crossed in front of you
- Sit upright, but don't stiffen your body|
- Let your hands drop to your sides
- Dropping your chin downwards, let your gaze fall gently down
- Relax

Meditation

- Relax, focus on your breathing... on how you feel
- Feel your breathe... Follow it .... goes in and out... pause on the outbreath
- Focus on the air moving through your nose or mouth, the rising of falling ... of your tummy or even your chest...
- You might find your attention move to other places when you realise your mind has wondered gently move it back to your breath.
- Stay present; your mind might wander off your breath, instead of wrestling with your thoughts just sit and pay attention. That is all there is... to learn to be...
- When you are ready.... lift your eyes and notice any sounds in the environment, how does your body feel right now?

Reflection

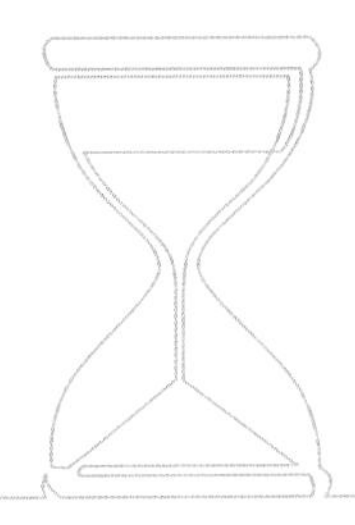

Why not reflect how you are feeling as you engage your practices.

WEEK #1 Think	Feel	Respond
WEEK #2 Think	Feel	Respond
WEEK #3 Think	Feel	Respond

Reflection

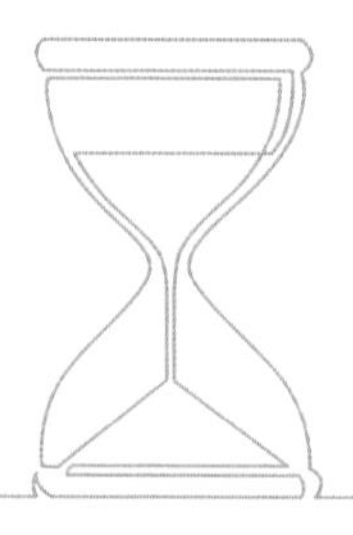

How are you feeling, thinking and responding...

WEEK #4 Think	Feel	Respond
WEEK #5 Think	Feel	Respond
WEEK #6 Think	Feel	Respond

Step 7

What drives you? Love or Fear?

The source that drives me...

In recent years I have realised that there are two sources we can plug into: Love or Fear. I have taught myself to recognise these sources, how they show up in me and shifting my source, a choice.

I know I am simplifying two very challenging topics yet it's a simple way to reflect on the emotions and intentions that drive us, drive how we see our world and interact with others.

Love is a place I call peace, presence, freedom, joy, honesty, discomfort yet safe, openness, courage, bravery, "grounded", worthiness, trust, faith, unburdened, naked, exposed, belief... When I come from a place of love, I can be curious, ask questions, not respond from a place of protection. I can set boundaries with others because I care enough for me. I can try new things and fail. I can be patient and not buy into fear ... I am compassionate and kind to others and am willing to build relationships without fear.

Fear for me is a place of great danger, of the worst happening, of being rejected, laughed at, it's a place where I am shamed and my failure impacts my entire life. It is a place where I protect myself, I cannot hear or see others. I only see my own "fear" coming to life. I live in the past and project this into the future. I am lonely, and keep others at arm's length. I am strong and yet I am brittle. I get angry and overwhelmed easily. I avoid feedback and judgment. I don't like myself and I am numb to my feelings.

I know I am no alone. I have learnt how to shift from fear to love; you can too! Yet you need to recognise the source that drives you. When you do, you need to choose to let go of fear .

"Our emotions dance in the paradox of love and fear."

Debasish Mridha

There is research behind love & fear!

Elisabeth Kübler-Ross, a highly acclaimed psychiatrist, is quoted saying that we have two raw emotions; Fear and Love. Based on her research, she found that all feelings we feel stem from either Love or Fear. Understanding the fundamental differences between these emotions will help us know when we are "plugged" into either emotion and make sure they don't control us.

When we can identify our raw root emotions what we are experiencing we can understand what we are feeling and why. Once we have done this, we can choose to deal with our feelings, recognise them for what they are, move past them if we want to, or if it serves us. We cannot be plugged into Love and Fear at the same time. If we choose one emotion, we can move out of another. If we know which emotions are Fear-based and which are Love based, we can choose to strive for Love when we are stuck in Fear

Love or Fear

Love

Unconditional Deep affection.
It is open and generous.
Allows us to be with others

Fear

Pulls us away from others. It's the belief that someone will cause us harm or pain or we are in danger.

Reference to Love and Fear: https://www.skilledatlife.com/why-we-need-to-know-that-all-emotions-stem-from-either-love-or-fea/r

HAPPINESS: Joy, Delight, Bliss, Pleasure Happiness comes when we let go of expectations and accept / welcome what we experience.

EMPATHY: Is deep connection with somone. When we allow ourselves to feel what someone is feeling and to place ourselves in their world. Compassion & kindness.

CERTAINTY: Accepting what will happen. Trusting faith that all will be how it should be. It looks like peaceful, excitement, selfcontrol, tranquility.

BELONGING: We feel part of a group. We belong to a group of similar interests, where even if we are different it's safe and accepted to bring what we have..

WONDER: Grateful for all we have Surprise, amazement and awe

ACCEPTANCE: Peace of Mind & calm. Relief, comfort, non-judgement, cooperation and contentment.

Fear looks like

GRIEF: Believe things are wrong, unfair It's the feeling that our expectations are not met and resisting to accept things as they are. depression, remorse, regret, despair, hopeless and disappointment

APATHY: No concern/ respect for others It's comes from isolation of self and no connection. hate, resentment, hosility

UNCERTAIN: We fear the unknown/ future Weary, distress, worry, anxiety, stress and doubt

SHAME: The intense feeling that we are flawed in some way that reflects on us not being good enough and accepted. Embarrassment, envy, disrespect, humiliation

HORROR: Intense Pain, impending doom. Can manifest itself as feelings of terror, hysteria, shock, panic, helplessness, alarm, fright or disbelief

ANGER: Is a feeling of being "wronged". Frustration, competitiveness, fury, bitterness and resentment

Reflection Recognising Love or Fear Emotions

Reflect on the emotions you are experiencing:

- Do you recognise your emotion?
- Is it serving you and allowing you to bring your best?
- What Is the emotion ...
- What story is your emotion telling you? One that you need to check?
- Is the emotion allowing you to be connected and to feel present?
- Is the emotion serving you?
- Are you willing to gently reframe the story, connect with yourself and shift your root emotion?

Reflection
Love & Fear

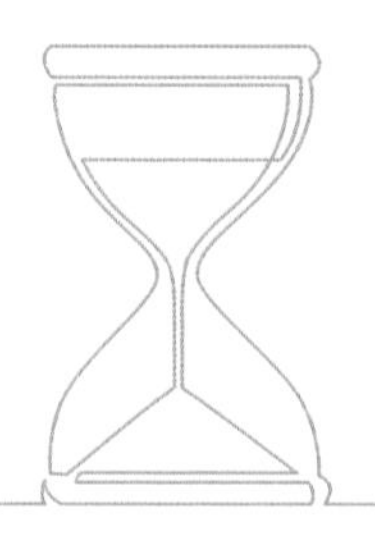

A few years ago, I was exhausted. My adrenal glands stopped working, and I was cautioned my stress was taking me to an early heart attack. I realise today I was living in **FEAR**. I had suffered trauma in my life that kept my brain in survival mode - plugged into **FEAR** more than **LOVE.**

I decided to work on Freedom and Peace because my fear held me captive. Fear had driven me to achieve, strive and compete. Yet some of the fear emotions no longer served me. Today I recognised when I am stuck in fear, I choose to move into **LOVE!** It takes courage to focus on reflecting. It takes choice and ownership to shift our source. It is liberating to live in **LOVE;** it will be a life journey for me.

What are the 5 emotional responses you have most frequently?

★ Consider the list shared earlier in this step.

Reflection

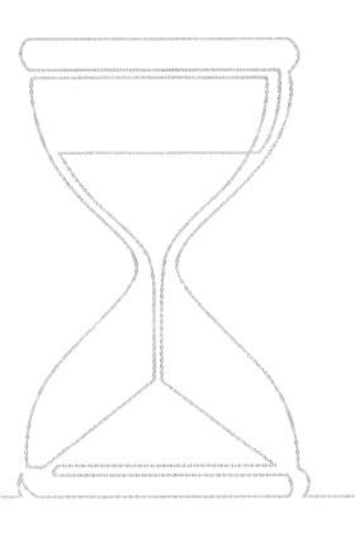

Why could shifting into LOVE more regularly help you ?

If you could show up your "Best self" what would your impact be?
Your behaviours?

Step 8

Freeing YOU!

Lets talk about Freeing you!

Ever feel like you can't be your "real" self? That you wrestle with how to be all you can be? Fear that what you have and who we are will be rejected or not accepted by others? Hold yourself back and stay small?

This leads to our EGO needing to operate in overdrive to protect us. As much as it powers us forward, It keeps us stuck. What causes our wrestle? Shame and our Fear hold the key.

Brene Brown talks about the gifts of imperfection and shares with us the worthiness areas that we can wrestle with, I have realised that she empowered so many of us with the toolkit to take down the bars of our "fear and life made" cages. The cages we create to protect ourselves, yet they disconnect us from bringing all we have.

So why do we wrestle with worthiness? Because we want to be connected, feel part of something bigger, feel like we are accepted with all our gifts and talents. As humans, the challenge is that we all wrestle with the fear of not being good enough, and the little voice of SHAME becomes the superglue of the cage that keeps us small. So accepting who we are and nurturing ourselves allows us to bring the best of what we have. Maybe the challenge is we don't even recognise who we really are. I remember at one stage I was so disconnected from me I didn't even know how to order a meal at a restaurant because
I didn't know what I liked? So being willing to look inside and freeing me is critical to live!

Meeting & understanding shame

Recently I used the word "shame" to explain to a friend what my journey has been and how I was responding to my world. They were not sure why I used the word "Shame".

I am going to remind you of how I define Shame. Dr Brene Brown studies human behaviour and why we get stuck in the destructive cycles we do. Why we struggle to live our best life; in her research, she came across SHAME. Shame keeps us wrestling with connection and with our imperfection. (our imperfection being what separates us because it means we are "faulty" - that is our story)

Shame is the intense feeling that we are flawed in some way. This flaw reflects on us not being good enough or accepted. We suffer the fear of connection, embarrassment, humiliation, intense disrespect. When we feel shame, we want to sink into the ground and disappear. We look inward and start to view ourself in a negative light.

When I realised that shame was causing my survival brain to go off like a new years eve fireworks show, I realised I needed to own it because it impacted how I was thinking, talking, engaging, and being.

"Shame is the most powerful, master emotion.
It's the fear that we're not good enough."
- BrenéBrown.

"You cannot shame or belittle people into changing their behaviours"
BrenéBrown

5 ways shame shows up in our lives

1 We avoid relationships, vulnerability and community. We hide and self-conceal who we are with the world. We hide from communities and friendships and vulnerability is a no-no.

2 We suppress our emotions. We are ashamed of who we are and keep our thoughts and feelings inside.

3 We could feel worthless, depressed and anxious; we have low selfesteem. When we are constantly ashamed, we have a daily emotional and mental battle.

4 We don't take decisions that could cause us to fail or leave us open to judgment. I could even avoid taking care of my health.

5 We could relapse into destructive behaviours. We don't believe healing or change is possible and want to numb how we feel. We believe we are worthless and can treat ourselves as worthless. We engage in behaviour we know are not aligned to our values or are bad for our health or well-being. Think of those destructive addictions that you might be connected too yet won't own!

Shame is the biggest cause of depression, anxiety, substance abuse, addiction (all kinds) and suicide. It can impact anyone. There is a way through, I found it...

Reference: www.clearviewtreatment.com

My Story

My story has so many "shame" triggers.
I am going to share a few with you...

I found my self molested as a 5-year-old child. (Breath deeply please). I never realised how this fundamentally changed my life. It was the start of the awful wrestle of worthiness that would eat away at my life for years and compound. It left a gaping hole in my self-worth that I needed to fill with that search for worthiness.

All I wanted was to be loved and accepted. Here is the crazy part, my parents and family so loved me, yet I felt dirty. I had a few other shame elements that ate away at my worthiness; I have an olive skin tone. I grew up in apartheid South Africa; I never felt I fitted in. I was denied toilet keys at a rest stop at the age of 8. The family sitting opposite us in the restaurant had a full conversation of whether we were white or of colour. I was so ashamed. My beautiful dad whom I look just like, kept me in the shade as much as possible to avoid my chocolate coloured tan that would cause ethnicity incidents. In my first marriage (yes my first) my then husband when intoxicated would ask his friends to "check my gums" as he taunted me for my colouring. (In South Africa when apartheid and segregation took place, it was a way to test which ethnicity you would be classed). The shame... oh the shame of being "flawed".

I hope you can imagine with me that shame bars were holding me captive. I am not alone in my shame... the bars that kept me locked inside, hiding... every imperfection became another story I told myself of why I should keep hidden and armour up!

Setting me free!

"Acceptance is the Ultimate act of courage"
Brené Brown

I have and still wrestle with vulnerability and worthiness. I recognise I am on a journey with so many. I am determined to free my brave self and learn to accept and embrace the imperfect parts of me. I am learning to own my shame and retell my story! It's brave and courage filled and ultimately freedom.

Shame is the story we tell ourselves that we are flawed and therefore not worthy of love and belonging...

How does shame grow? Shame grows in secrecy, silence, and judgment. Thank you, Dr Brené Brown, for your research. Let me tell you who judges us first, that little voice in our own head, the one that yells out our shame in messages of worthlessness. You are not good enough; you are a failure, you won't be loved if this came out, you will be rejected for life, you are bad. You don't belong.

We need to remember that we can retell our story; we can have the courage to be seen, to rise. We can have compassion and kindness for ourselves, and we can lay the armour down that hold us captive in shame and keep us from being free! Being all we can, creative, open, filled with joy.

"Because true belonging only happens when we present our authentic, imperfect selves to the world, our sense of belonging can never be greater than our level of self-acceptance."
Brené Brown

5 ways to unlock the shame cage & start living

1 Find safe relationships and be vulnerable. Find a community where you can be yourself, shame disappears in a shared safe space.

2 Get shame into the sunlight. Move it from in your head to the open Write your story of shame, share it creatively, speak about it to help others. Shame heals when exposed. Remember to share with those you trust.

3 Start loving you! Have compassion for yourself, Speak to you with love and care as you would to a dear friend. Love yourself for your imperfections, care for yourself, be kind to you. (Speak lovingly to yourself!)

4 Take a risk that could expose you to shame. I am dyslexic and I am writing human stories and this guide. I am taking a risk and bringing what I have. It's the only way to be free!

5 Believe you can heal from shame. Start with one small decision in the right direction and believe you can make better decisions again and again. Like when I shift from FEAR TO LOVE, I choose it for me and those I love (Myself included in the LOVE!)

I want to add one more thing, knowing how you behave when your shame triggers go off, acknowledging that this isn't the "me you want to be" and being willing to own your present and future is so important. This will allow you to start undoing the shame cage that keeps you small, hidden and hurting! I love the thought that we can see it, own it, solve it and do it (Thank you OZ principle!)

Reflection

Consider the 5 ways to unlock your shame cage, what reflections do you have from these? Where could you start?

What support might you need to help you work through your shame? Who is in your trust circle that you can speak too? What does courage look like for you?

Step 9

Put the shame bag down!

Being free from shame is a journey, like peeling an onion!

Do you remember my opening welcome? I mentioned that growing "me" wasn't a miracle fix! Working to free me from the cage that keeps me small is a one day at a time learning journey. The importance of creating practices that help calm your brain is a critical component of success. The second is to make sure you hear the stories you are telling yourself and remember you are not your thoughts!

Now, of course, it has taken excruciating experiences to help solidify your cage. So it would be realistic to note that you will have moments where something will happen in your day and before you can catch yourself you are responding with armour, and you have PICKED UP YOUR SHAME...

Consider the CAGE analogy I used in step 8. Imagine when your trigger goes off, and you are still working on owning this shame and fear that is based on a belief, experience and is very real... that shame bar you worked so hard on will swing back into place to protect you. You will slip into keeping the "me you want to be" small and locked inside and take on the strong, hard and tough persona you have created. Inside you are in pain and those messages of unworthiness are playing in the back of your mind like a hit song on repeat!

How do we get through, keep the bars down and stay free? Well, it's a journey of acceptance and the willingness to not avoid our fear and shame but to look it in the eye, see it and thank it for trying to take care of you and then choosing to let go. I think that might be harder than anything I have had to do..

Reflection Putting shame bags down!

What "shame" stories do you carry around?

What are your triggers to picking up your "shame bag"?

What practices can you take to be more accepting?

What new story might you tell yourself?

Who can you connect with to: - Own your story & behavior?

- Be accepted for who you are?

- Be challenged to put your bag down?

Notes

References
& recommended readings

Achor, Shawn (2011) *The Happiness Advantage: The Seven Principles of Positive Psychology that Fuel Success and Performance at Work*

Brown, Brené (2010) *The Gifts of Imperfection - Let Go of Who You Think You're Supposed to Be and Embrace Who You Are*

Brown, Brené (2010) *The Wholehearted Inventory - This instrument assesses your strengths and opportunities for growth www.brenebrown.com/wholeheartedinventory*

Chamine, Shirzad (2012) *Positive Intelligence: Why Only 20% of Teams and Individuals Achieve Their True Potential AND HOW YOU CAN ACHIEVE YOURS*

Maxwell, John C. (2014) *The 15 Invaluable Laws of Growth: Live them and reach your potential*

Tolle, Eckhart (2004) *The Power of Now: A Guide to Spiritual Enlightenment*

Resources,
books & tools

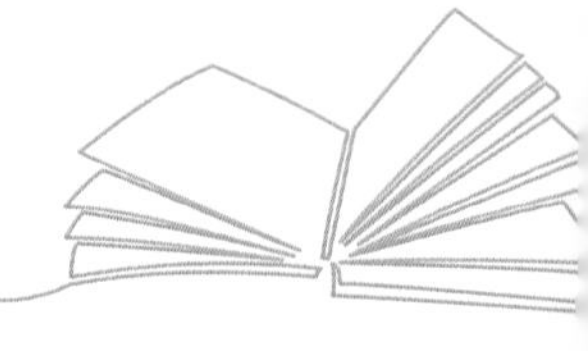

Online resource hub - The Culture Hive
This portal has resources (videos & articles) to guide and support your growth and insight into yourself as well as leadership and high performing cultures. Visit **www.ignitepurpose.com.au/culture-hive** and download any of the three areas of growth you feel are right for you.

Growth tools - The Ignite Shop
We have designed tools to aide you in your journey of growth and reflection,. These tools include self-care cards, sand timer to remind you to take time out, mindfulness bracelets to help you stay present, and so much more! **Visit www.ignitepurpose.com.au/shop-ignite-purpose**

Podcast Channels
We have two podcast channels available

- **Ignite purpose with Christina Foxwell** is a program to celebrate being humans together and listening to people sharing their stories.
  Available on Spotify or **www.anchor.fm/christina-foxwell**

- **Grow Me** is a program to support your growth and development and supplement this GrowMe Guide
  Available on Spotify or **https://anchor.fm/christina-foxwell6**

Final thoughts...

Thank you for growing you; I am grateful you have managed to read, reflect, heal and grow throughout this book, the first of many. I have shared the foundation for growing ME and the importance of understanding who you are and how to rewire your brain and unlock you!

I would encourage you to:

- Start having a deep relationship with YOU
- Be kind to yourself so that you can be kind to others
- Your imperfection is beautiful, embrace it
- Working on YOU is the biggest gift you can give yourself

In the work I do we support culture growth, leadership development and align people. I need to acknowledge that growth and change starts with each person. This is always the key, so to be happy, fulfilled, successful, connected, it must start with how you live, lead and love.

In Book 2, I will be sharing how to FREE YOU so that you can be better with others and win together. How you can step into compassion, empathy and how you can learn to develop your LOVE and WISE self.

If you have had the courage to start the journey with me in this guide, please persavere and continue to grow. The more you grow, the more growth you will find you need. It's not a race; it's a meandering of being present in your own life as you embrace actually LIVING! I will keep saying this, we are not better alone, we are better together, and it only happens when we can learn to work on who we are and heal. You will find that you judge less, stay more present and start unlocking the ME you want to be.

Christina Foxwell